Paddle
WHISPERS

Paddle
WHISPERS

written and illustrated by
DOUGLAS WOOD

 Pfeifer-Hamilton

Pfeifer-Hamilton Publishers
210 West Michigan
Duluth MN 55802-1908
218-727-0500

Paddle Whispers

Printed in the United States of America by Versa Press Inc.
10 9 8 7 6 5 4 3 2 1

Publisher: Donald A Tubesing
Editorial Director: Susan Gustafson
Assistant Editor: Patrick Gross
Art Director: Joy Morgan Dey

Library of Congress Cataloging in Publication Data
92-61330

ISBN 0-938586-73-4

Dedicated
To James and Joyce, Dorris and Blanche,
who gave me the North Woods.
To Sig, who blazed a trail and encouraged
me to blaze my own.
To Kathy, as lovely as the sunrise,
and as true.

*Special thanks for the
preparation of this manuscript
and artwork to:
Corrine Dwyer
Joy Morgan Dey
Kathy Wood
Susan Gustafson
The late J. Arnold Bolz*

*Believe one who knows; you will find something
greater in woods than in books.
Trees and stones will teach you that which you can
never learn from masters.*

—St. Bernard de Clairvaux, 1115 A.D.

*I have learned a lot from trees;
Sometimes about the weather,
Sometimes about animals,
Sometimes about the Great Spirit.*

—Walking Buffalo

Foreword

I began writing these thoughts for myself, in order to understand a landscape. Two landscapes, really—that of the North, the great swath of rock, forest, and water that has held me in its spell since childhood, and that of my own life. I wanted to ponder the landmarks I found—the meanings within island and stream, storm and sunrise, boulder and moccasin flower.

In such a search, one travels alone. But along the way I often found the markings of others who had been there before me—a blaze along the trail, a small stack of split wood beside an old campsite.

Later, as I continued writing and sketching, I talked with many who had taken similar journeys. Or planned to. Or someday hoped to. We shared notes and maps, talked of dreams and fears, rapids and portages, and of the still, small secrets of the woods.

Somewhere along the way these thoughts clarified, and became my own markings along the trail—a bent twig perhaps, some firewood . . . I leave them with care, that they don't obstruct the beauty of the landscape. And with a simple wish for those who find them. Good journey . . .

Douglas Wood
August 1992

Trying to catch the meanings that were there, in that moment before the lifting of the dark.

—Sigurd F. Olson

Going in ...

Dawn in the North Woods. The silence of rocks. A sleeping lake, wrapped in night blankets of fog. The paddle whispers, the canoe glides. From far ahead I hear rising the long, lone wail of a single loon.

From where the loon calls, an outlet. A phantom river lost in fog and bulrushes. Finally, a break in the rushes, an almost imperceptible current swirls past a great boulder, a black finger of water points into the mist.

The paddle whispers,
the canoe glides . . .

*F*rom green-black walls of forest begin to float the first madrigals—white-throated sparrows and hermit thrushes and veeries. A heron flaps ahead into the mist, settles, moves again. A kingfisher swoops close by, then rattles from a dead branch.

The sun climbs over the pines. Over the spruces. Over Saganaga, Kabetogama, Nistowiak, Namew, Athabaska. And ten thousand other places with no names.

The North Woods calls. The river pulls, the paddle whispers. I listen. And gradually . . . gradually the mist burns away.

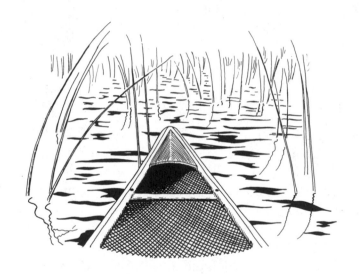

Riverbanks lined with green trees, fragrant grasses: A place not sacred? Where?

—Zen Forest Sayings

But how to truly explore this land of poetry and storms and solitude, of lakes and islands more beautiful than dreams? I want to listen more deeply than ever before to its secrets and catch its meanings, and at the same time, perhaps, my own.

Yet such things can't be sought out or thought out, captured or even discovered. They come, if they come at all, quietly, unplanned, almost unnoticed. Like the rustling of an aspen in the wind, tracks on the beach left by small creatures in the night, or a shaft of sunlight slanting down through a vaulted cathedral of pines.

These will be my landmarks. And perhaps through the accumulation of them, a whole landscape will emerge.

The river pulls. An unseen lake calls. The paddle whispers, the canoe glides . . .

I hold in my hand a small chunk of cedar, and absently whittle at the bark as I gaze upon a blue shield of lake, bossed with emerald islands and the sailing reflections of clouds. It is midday, and I sit in the shade of an old white pine, my back against its trunk. The air is sweet with the scent of dry needles. Among the pine's spreading roots, delicate harebells sway with an imperceptible breeze. Down a slope of granite, the canoe is moored among sedges and leatherleaf, and the lake is whispering secrets to the shore. I gaze at the horizon, whittle at the cedar.

The bark is soon gone, and I have created . . . have arrived at . . . a new surface. How far would I have to go, I wonder, before running out of surfaces? Out of horizons? To the heartwood? To the quark? To the quasar?

I whittle off a few more shavings and stuff them into my pocket, tinder for the evening fire. I untie the canoe and push off from shore, pointing the bow toward a distant island.

Under every surface is another surface; beyond each horizon, a wider horizon. I whittle. I explore. And sometimes just rest. In the cool, scented shade of mystery.

I only went out for a walk, and finally concluded to stay out until sundown; for going out, I found, was really going in.

—JOHN MUIR

Markings...

*E*vening, and first camp. A late cup of sweetgale tea, the leaves gathered from along the shore. The evening star begins to shine as if it means to challenge the moon, and the moon, just a sliver, begins to slide down a dark blue slope of western sky. Shadows lengthen and fling themselves across silvered water. A loon begins to wail and pauses in mid-lonesome; a barred owl hoots from the black shoreline across the lake.

The North is singing all her old songs—even the whine of the mosquitoes that eventually drive me into the safety of the tent. There I pull out a flashlight and spread the maps, retracing the pattern of routes once taken, plotting those to come. A good map is essential for any journey into the bush; but more than that, it becomes a companion and a trusted friend. Even long after the trip is over, a map can be spread out and, in an instant, rekindle memories seemingly forgotten—a birch-clad shoreline mirrored in wine-colored water, the sting of wind-driven spray from a wild nor'easter, the smell of incense from balsam twigs tossed onto a campfire.

My map is, of course, a symbol, a picture of some terrain. What it is not is the terrain itself. This distinction seems obvious, but it's easy to forget, for I live in a world of symbols—words, pictures, numbers, images, broadcasts—all constituting a sort of map, a description of the landscape of life. But not the landscape itself.

The map I have spread on the tent floor has, in itself, no real value, and no meaning. Like any map, it is of value only insofar as it enables me to *experience* the real world.

It is this experience I am after on this solitary quest, this adventure of the spirit. But now, alone in the night, gazing at the map and the lakes, rivers, and portages to come, I feel a pang of doubt, and I wonder . . . Am I ready? For the aloneness, the decisions, the occasional dangers of storm and wind and rapids? Are there answers waiting in the wilderness, or will I merely wander into new thickets of questions?

I know only that it is my journey to make, that ultimately I alone am responsible—for pulling the paddle, for feeling the moist duff or hard granite under my feet, for seeing the sparkle of the water and watching the sun rise over a dark hill, and for walking, silent and alert, down some gently calling forest trail. And I know that if I look and listen closely enough, what I find will be what is there.

The moon is gone, the night is still. The mosquitoes have subsided. I slip outside for one last listen, stand under the ink-black shape of a pine, fill my lungs with the night scent of the North. The North . . . with its dark and silent mantle of forest draped over the shoulders of the continent. A land of many moods and many names. The *bois forts*, or strong woods, of the early French explorers. The boreal forest, the Laurentian shield, the Canadian shield. The North Woods. The *pays d'en haut.*

Home, they say, is where your dreams live. And despite my doubts about the journey I have begun, I know that, for me, there is no better name for this country that has enchanted me for so long. Tonight, with glaciated granite underfoot and stars overhead, I am home.

The water chuckles almost inaudibly at the shore. In the west there seems to be a ragged bank of black beneath the stars. It could blow later. I check the canoe, making sure that it's snugged safely and the paddles are secure. I go back into the tent, fold up the maps. From far down-lake a loon once more casts a voice to the shores and the silence and, this time, finishes the hymn.

I think over again my small adventures;
my fears,
Those small ones that seemed so big;
For all the vital things
I had to get and to reach,
And yet there is only one great thing,
The only thing:
To live to see the great day that dawns
And the light that fills the world.

—OLD INUIT SONG

Morning dawns full of crystal light and the arias of song sparrows and veery thrushes. It's a sparkling sapphire of a day, the lake glistening with a thousand flagships of the sun. The storm must have gone around, and the doubts of last night now seem equally far away.

I make breakfast, clean up, break camp, move down the lake.

The paddle whispers,
the canoe glides . . .

*M*ore sunrises. More moonrises. A string of campfires glowing in the dark. Days and lakes that slip slowly away like the whirlpools that spin away from the paddle. Beauty seeps in.

It is early afternoon, and as I paddle along a series of looming cliffs, a pattern has been established. Clouds continually form and build in the west, then go around— to the south, to the north. Occasionally I catch a few drops of rain from the edge of a shower. But suddenly the pattern changes. Almost unbelievably fast, a squall line sweeps across the lake, driving a black wall of rain before it. White caps leap like wolves. There's nothing along this shore but rock! Quick, if I can just get behind this little point . . . There! Now pull the canoe up and scramble for the ledge with the overhang. *Please* don't let lightning hit this rock.

Wind tears. Thunder slams. A searing flash and an ancient skeleton of pine shatters not sixty feet away.

Fear. Humility. Awareness—no, *Aliveness.* They seem to go together.

Without a house or a building for shelter, rain is personal. Without a tent, it's even more personal. Squatting on a narrow ledge ducking lightning bolts, you *are* the rain. You are the storm and the rock and the crashing waves, and the entire universe is suddenly *very* personal.

I think this will be a good experience, if I survive it.

Squalls like this don't usually last very long. Sooner or later, it's got to stop.

Later.

No matter how cold and wet you are, you're always warm and dry.

—OLD WOODSMAN'S (LIE) ADAGE

Sometimes . . . at the end of a stormy day, or in the middle of a big lake . . . there is an island. Round and whole, magical and serene, small enough to comprehend but large enough to accommodate the spirit, it is a tiny mirror of the cosmos.

An island. It can be a place, it can be an idea, or even a hope. But for a short while, at least, it is somewhere to rest, to renew the joy of being, to gather strength for the journey.

A place to watch the winds turn. And the days turn. And the stars turn.

I sit on a rock at the end of the island, peeling off flakes of sunburned nose. Feet dangle in cool water; minnows nibble at toes. Overhead a broad-winged hawk sends a thin whistle, her voice too small for her size. She traces invisible circles on a canvas of robin's-egg blue.

I have my own circles to trace. But for now I don't move. Everything depends, I guess, on how you spend your time, yet there are times when *not doing* is the most important thing *to do*. When the me on the rock sits a little more definitely with each slow circle of the hawk, and the not-me floats away, unnoticed even by minnows.

"But what," badgers a relentless voice, "exactly are you doing out here? What are you accomplishing? What are you getting out of it? And what, oh especially what are you going to do with your life?"

The voice usually stops me. Knocks me down, kicks sand in my face. But this time, finally, I tell the voice to shut up. It's a stupid question, what are you going to do with your life. Setting out to do something with your life is like sitting down to eat a moose. Nobody ever did anything successfully with their life. Instead they did something with their day. Each day.

Sunrise is birth. Sleep is death. Each day *is your life*. Let the moose run. Eat some blueberries.

Each day comes to me with both hands full of possibilities, and in its brief course I discern all the verities and realities of my existence; the bliss of growth, the glory of action, the spirit of beauty.

—HELEN KELLER

And the lake breathes . . . and the timeless rhythms of the earth ebb and flow . . . and on my island, I am still . . .

From the stillness, eventually, eyes and thoughts reach once more to a far shore. It is time to go. I have been here long enough, have made the acquaintance of every stone and every tree. I know the stunted red pine that holds the sun when it sets, and the little speckled alder on the point where the song sparrow has her nest. I know the dome of granite where the corydalis blooms, and the offshore rockpile where the gulls stand and cry as if they wept for the world. I know the root I trip over by the tent, and the hollow where the sphagnum moss is damp and soft, and the sloping ledge where the canoe lies, waiting . . .

The paddle whispers,
the canoe glides . . .

$\mathcal{I}$'m sure there are many things I'll never learn from traveling over the earth by canoe. I'm just not sure any of them are worth much.

With a canoe, it's simple. An empty bow always swings with the wind. Lean too far and you tip over. When you don't paddle, you drift. When you do paddle, keep your bow lined up on the horizon, or you'll go in circles. Don't over-pack, you have to carry all you bring. Scout a rapids before you run it. When paddling, it sometimes helps to sing a song, but be quiet if you want to see and hear shy things . . .

Sometimes the best paddling is in the evening. If the wind's been stiff during the day, or if I want to see a moose, or a beaver. Or fly among the reflections of stars. Or just smell the cool sweetness of the earth.

Tonight I paddle by the North Star. It's a gentle spark, not nearly as bright as the planets. But it is constant, while they wander. Constellations—Cassiopeia, Draco, the Great and Little Bear—spin around it, turning with hour and season. But the North Star is still, a beacon for anyone on a journey through the night.

And if I keep letting it shine into me, for nights and nights and years and years, maybe one night I'll shine back. Constant. Steady.

All things are symbols: the external shows of Nature have their image in the mind . . . .

—HENRY WADSWORTH LONGFELLOW

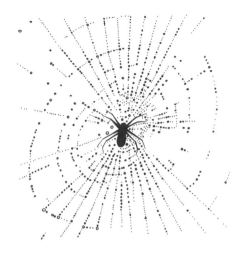

*O*n a damp gray morning beside a stream, I watch a
spider spin a web. She is very small. She spins from a
spruce twig to my jacket pocket, then back again. She
spins one filament, then another. Another. And I follow a
thin thread of reverie—a realization that, to this little
spinner, I am just one more convenient rock. A plaid
stump. Thoughts, dreams, motivations—all the things
that make me, *me*—to spider, these are merest rumors.
Immaterial. Unreal.

But when I finally stir, when I rise and break the
web and turn spider's world on end, it is because of these
phantom qualities that I move. My inner world has
changed her outer world, as hers has first done to mine.
The greater reality is unseen, unheard, perhaps undreamed. That which moves all things is on the inside.

Walking along the stream, I notice what I somehow missed before. The spider webs are everywhere. Exquisite webs, hundreds of them—every stunted jack pine and ground juniper gilded with a necklace, each necklace hung with lucent pearls of dew. And, whispering in the first breeze, an old question of the night: What of *my* webs? What are my choices, my chances; how much effort should really be spent on such fragile, ephemeral enterprises, sure to be blown away by some wild wind, or torn up by some plaid jacketed clodhopper? To what end all the spinning, the careful planning, the anchoring? The striving for beauty?

An opaline sun begins to pierce the mist, and the necklaces glisten, and from some dream-secret spinner comes reply: They are happiest who are tied at many levels and in many ways to the world around them. *Expand yourself,* says the spinner. *Grow, reach, risk, invest, incorporate more of the universe into your world. Spin, spin . . .*

The water lily opens to the sun. The pine spreads its
arms into the sky. The trickle flows into the stream, flows
into the river, flows into the ocean. Flows into the cloud.
All living, growing things flow, move toward openness.
And nothing is ever lost . . .

The paddle whispers,
the canoe glides . . .

portage . . . *the carrying of boats or goods overland from one body of water to another; the route followed in making such a transfer.*

—WEBSTER'S NEW COLLEGIATE DICTIONARY

*T*here are, I believe, only three kinds of people in the world. There are the ones who have said, "Yes." There are the ones who have said, "No." And there are the ones who haven't noticed a question yet.

I have a canoe on my head, a rock in my shoe, mosquitoes up my pants, blackflies burrowing into my neck, and beaver bog water running down my backside. And I think this must be today's version of the question.

But if I have it figured right, there are only about two hundred and ninety steps to go on this portage trail, and at the end of it is a cold, blue lake that's going to feel about one thousand times better than the best shower I've ever had.

If it's true as Socrates once said that "the unexamined life is not worth living," then it's equally true that the unlived life is not worth examining.

That's if I have it figured right.

Ah, I did.

. . . But I wonder if I'll regret not taking my clothes off first.

*I*s there any one thing in the world as personally unrewarding as pulling on a pair of wet jeans first thing in the morning? Anything even approaching the pure despair of it? This is awful. This is torture. This is . . .

Wait. Isn't that a white-throated sparrow singing from the little island, his song so pure it aches? And from over in the cedars, there's a winter wren warbling like flowing water. A Swainson's thrush is singing down a rain barrel somewhere back in the woods, and—well now, the whole morning is drenched in bird songs. Morning ghosts of mist are racing across the water, and, down the lake, a flaming sun is throwing a leg up over the hills.

Now I remember—I'm camping out in the universe. Campsite, Earth. Cold-hot, dry-wet, green-blue, miserable-wonderful, *real* Earth. And she's alive. And so am I.

The woods were made for the hunters of dreams,
the brooks for the fishers of song . . .

—SAM WALTER FOSS

The paddle whispers,
the canoe glides . . .

*T*oday was filled with pelicans—fishing in the swirl-ing currents under the waterfalls, sailing along the shore-lines. I came to a small island, covered as though by a white blanket. I paddled close, and the blanket lifted at one corner, undulated for a moment, and they were airborne . . .

Incredibly awkward and ungainly on solid ground, these great birds are transformed in flight into magical figures of grace, riding the thermals, gliding, banking, appearing and disappearing in the sun. Tonight as I drift toward sleep, my mind is filled with pelicans—spiraling, soaring pelicans. And with a wondering: Is life itself not flight? A series of outrageous, gravity-defying maneuvers produced in combination with, because of, and in spite of all that is beyond us and within us, to which the only appropriate response can be—to dance. Impossibly. Beautifully. In mid-air.

Morning. A single cloud in a blue sky. A breeze through the aspens. A wave on the water. A canoe, a paddler. A dance.

The paddle whispers,
the canoe glides . . .

*R*ain. Three days of rain. A sodden world of trembling leaves and dripping needles, the invariable background hush-h-h-h of raindrops on the water. No songs of birds. No chuckling of wavelets. Iron sky. Black lake. Lowering clouds of mist. And I gradually notice that my mind is wrapped in its own cold mist of . . . loneliness. Not the normal, mostly pleasant solitude of a solo canoe trip, but a feeling of isolation. Of being disconnected. I'm surprised that it reminds me so much of the feeling one can get in a strange and busy city, or in a crowded room—a sense of separateness, of somehow not being a part of . . .

Out on the lake, silver globes of lake water leap into the air where the raindrops hit. I sit on a boulder and watch. After a long time, I notice beside the boulder a little balsam fir. Elegant, graceful, glistening in raindrops, she rises from the inch-thick duff, standing in ten thousand years of eroded rock and dead lichens and mosses, pine, spruce, and balsam needles, the bodies of birches and cedars and voles and red squirrels and wolves.

And within the calligraphy of straight trunk, upswept branches, and feathery needles is composed a simple, eloquent statement: I haven't come into this place, I have grown *out* of it. I am connected, a part of all that has come before, and what comes after. I am daughter, sister, mother, grandmother. I am here. I am life.

A little rivulet of rainwater winds past the balsam, through the duff, past my feet, and down the granite to the lake. Away with it flows loneliness.

Overhead on a limb, a red squirrel has a pine cone. Within the seeds of a single cone, a sleeping forest.

Now what? Is the squirrel in the forest? Or is the forest in the squirrel?

In the light of understanding, you will see the entire creation within your own soul.

—THE BHAGAVAD-GITA

The paddle whispers,
the canoe glides . . .

It's evening, and I've come to a lovely little rock island, clad in spruce and cedar. Someone's used it as a campsite before, but not for a long time. The moss and lichens are untrampled, the tent site sprouted with bunchberry and wild sarsaparilla. Next to a band of rose quartz running through the bedrock are the stones of an old fire ring—mostly schist, with layered mica burnished gold by the heat of a long ago campfire. And over to one side, under a hanging spruce bough, lies a small stack of split wood, a scrap of birch bark still tucked under one corner . . .

After setting up the tent, I go down to the shore. The water ripples darkly. I scoop a kettleful and stop to listen. The lake laps gently at my feet. From a far shore etched with silhouettes of pines comes the deep, rhythmic challenge of a barred owl. In the northwest the last glow of day is fading, and the evening star has begun to shine. Two loons are throwing songs at it. The lake is wine. The evening is overfull with beauty.

I take the kettle of water back to the fire ring, and move the stones around to account for a slight breeze out of the north. The last time it must have been from the west. I'm careful to keep the stones off the band of quartz, just as they were. I wonder about the traveler who last camped here. What he heard and saw. And felt. I think back on the many journeys I've made with others, the many campfires I've shared, and how often I've sensed the strange truth that, even together, we each travel alone. But as I take one of the old sticks of kindling and slice off a pile of curled shavings for tinder, as I take the scrap of birch bark and strike a match to it, and the incense of cedar fills the night air, I know . . . even alone, we travel together.

In the morning I explore the island more completely, and after circling it, arrive once more at the band of rose quartz. It comes up from the water's edge, amid bushes of fragrant sweet gale and leatherleaf, and winds its way through the granite and schist on the point of the island. The vein sparkles with crystals the color of pasture rose petals. An igneous intrusion, geologists call it. A place where a molten finger of lava once flowed, pushing its way through a crack in the already existing bedrock, the pink color a result of contact with iron seepage from a subterranean hematite deposit.

Intrusion. An odd word for so beautiful a phenomenon, something so integrally a part of the North. It makes me wonder how much of the beauty of my own life I often miss by thinking of it as . . . intrusion. Like most people, I guess, the bedrock of my world is laced with intrusions, a seemingly endless supply of annoyances, interruptions, and distractions, small and large

problems that often seem to distort or overwhelm the conformations of my life.

And so I try to keep a feel for what's important and what's not; to simplify, like Thoreau; to keep a clean, hard outcrop of bedrock under my feet. Which is probably good. But the vein of rose quartz reminds me it's often the intrusions that give to life its color, its sparkle and its beauty. The intrusions can become a part of the bedrock, and, if they were all removed, what would be left—a perfect, seamless whole, or a broken assortment of unfilled cracks?

The paddles whispers,
the canoe glides . . .

There is no fairer subject for a picture than a pine. But the pine is the better artist; it paints pictures of the wind.

*P*ale pink corydalis. So delicate it looks as if it can hardly stand. Yet it blooms in the strangest of places. Not in some sheltered deposit of rich soil, but on the bedrock shoulders of windswept islands and shorelines. There it absorbs the full fury of Nor'easters, the spume of storm waves and the baking of summer sun, the rock-breaking frost of winter.

To everything it is exposed and, through it all, survives, a splash of pink tipped with yellow, adding carelessly to the beauty of things. And blooming in the strangest of places. Not just on the bedrock, but for anyone who has known it and glimpsed its meanings, in the heart as well.

Many men go fishing all their lives without knowing that it is not fish they are after.

—HENRY DAVID THOREAU

The paddle whispers,
the canoe glides . . .

*T*he Forecast:

There is a 95% chance that today's weather will be either too hot, too cold, too sunny, too rainy, or too windy.
From a desktop sign, Quetico Park Visitors Center

In many ways, a canoe trip is an endlessly repeated exercise in various modes of misery, each one a contrast—therefore, a relief, albeit temporary—to the misery preceding it. So there is always the illusion of looking forward to something that will most likely be . . . another misery.

A canoe trip could in fact be described as paddling—paddling until arms ache, back hurts, skin is burned, legs are cramped, and butt falls asleep. Finally, a portage and a chance to stop paddling, stretch legs, and get out of the sun. Also a chance to deal with blackflies, deerflies, and various other versions of evil incarnate; a chance to climb up and down hills with loads that would crush a burro, that strain neck, back, and hamstrings and threaten to drive shoulder blades through hips; a chance to wade through mud, muck, and other corruption, to climb over and under deadfalls and trip over stuff and to figure that death will probably arrive—mercifully—before this infernal trail reaches sight of blue, open, sunlit water. Where, of course, the cycle begins again.

The great goal and end of this particular cycle is the evening camp, that blessed spot of rock and tree kissed by evening breezes and the last slanted rays of the sun. Having found the camp, at whatever stage of exhaustion seems appropriate to the lateness of the hour and rigors of the day, it is time to set up the tent, gather wood, gather water, start a fire, get out the food, cook the food, and . . . ahhh . . . eat. And drink. In a warm and happy trance of pure bliss and satisfaction. This lasts . . . some moments. With the arrival of the evening watch of mosquitoes, the cooking gear is up-gathered and washed; the food repacked; the pack hoisted and hung safe from bears, mini-bears (chipmunks), and micro-bears (mice); personal hygiene is attended to; the tent entered; tent-invading mosquitoes dispatched (except for three which are never found); the sleeping bag snuggled into and finally, sleep. The sweet, dark, wonderful nothingness of . . . Rock. Root. Pinecone. These are nemeses that will be there, along with the three renegade mosquitoes, all through the night. They will become intimate with back, sides, and stomach, with muscles, bones, and insides— and loom ever larger and sharper and more offensive in the imagination and the anatomy, until dawn cannot come too soon.

And with the arrival of dawn—the pack is lowered (mini-bears found it anyway), breakfast cooked, dishes cleaned, tent taken down, the canoe loaded, and—back to paddling once more.

*T*he Backcast:

So why . . . why go through it? Why even be here?

The second answer is easy. Because "here" is where the beauty is. Here is where the sunsets are. Here is where the campsites and campfires are, and the clear, deep waters, and the loons, and the pines, and the islands. And yes, the storms and the big winds and the rapids. Here is where the *journey* is.

But why go through it? Why do I . . . why do *I* go through it? I think because no one else can go through it for me. And because the modern city-world system uses people to get work done. Important work, supposedly. That's the whole idea. That's why we get paid. But here—here *I'm* using work . . . to get myself done. What better work is there than that?

Or maybe . . . maybe it's enough to say that I am here, as another voyageur once put it, "to iron out the wrinkles in my soul."

And maybe it is only on the trail to nowhere-in-particular that you find the most important thing of all. Yourself.

Coming, going, the waterfowl
Leaves not a trace,
Nor does it need a guide.

—ZEN HAIKU

The paddle whispers,
the canoe glides . . .

*T*his morning I received yet another lesson in paddling a rapids. Actually it's the same lesson, many times over—that after all is said and done, there are really just two ways to do it. One way is to attack the water with skill and strength, making the canoe do what you want it to do. This is *fun*. For a while. Unfortunately this approach ignores the skill and strength of the rapids, which is almost always more skillful and stronger than you, and which has its own goals and plans for the canoe.

The other approach is to notice, to appreciate, the water and how it works, attuning yourself to its flow and positioning yourself to let it help you do what you need to do. This way is smarter. It's also drier. So why is it so hard to remember?

*T*his old portage trail symbolizes all the trails of the North—the rich smells of duff and moist earth, the mud holes in the seeps and low places, the exposed rocks and the roots worn smooth by countless heavy-laden steps from the past. And scattered along the trailsides, many an old friend, some who nod in greeting as I pass, others who carpet the rocks or bloom in the shadows or in the sunlit open glades.

As I move along, tossing silent hellos here and there, a literary question comes to mind: "What's in a name?"

Well, romance maybe. And conjurings. Intimations of beauty, perceived by other minds in other times . . .

Pipsissewa. Goldthread. Maidenhair. Indian Pipe. Meadowsweet. Ladyslipper. Blue Flag. Kinnikinnick. Wintergreen. Starflower. Snowberry.

And a trail through the woods becomes a walk through a poem.

Away, away, from men and towns,
To the wildwoods and the doons—
To the silent wilderness.

—PERCY BYSSHE SHELLY

It is evening, perhaps an hour of daylight left. The glassy lake is dimpled with rising fish, the distant shore a dim lavender balustrade of pines. All bathed in a soft, translucent light, pure as the first dawn. The day was swift with racing clouds, but now all is still. Still. Even the evening hymns of birds are for the moment absent. The thrushes and grosbeaks, the loon, the vireo—silent.

I have long loved the voices and songs, the poetry, I've found in the wilderness. But in this moment, this eternity of stillness, a simple truth is clear. Sometimes the most beautiful songs are unsung, the loveliest poems unspoken. In silence is equilibrium, poise, balance. Silence is, itself, a voice.

Woe unto them that join house to house, that lay field to field, till there be no place that they may be placed alone in the midst of the earth.

—Isaiah 5:8

The paddle whispers,
the canoe glides . . .

*T*his morning, it's just the smell. A north wind, and the smell of hundreds, thousands of miles of pine and spruce and balm of Gilead, of bare, glaciated rock, the spume of waterfalls and rapids and waves, the aroma of marshes and bogs and meadows and deep, deep woods.

It's the scent—the breath—of the earth itself, primeval. Nothing, save the call of the loon, so epitomizes the spirit of the North.

I breathe it in deeply, down to my toes, trying to savor every ingredient, every nuance. And I remember it was this same smell that I first fell in love with, long ago. Everything else followed—the places, the sights, the sounds, the journeys. But it was that first breath of the North Woods—so personal, so private, so unexpected—that caught me. It still does.

A tall tree reaches for the sun. A human mind reaches for—meaning, beauty, wholeness. Perhaps they are not so different, these two exertions, of tree, of mind. Perhaps they are not even separate processes at all. But after all the accumulated storms and droughts of life—pain, failure, loss—how does one continue to reach for such ideals, to believe in the possibility of attaining them? Sometimes I have wondered if I could continue to reach, and, looking at the tree, have seen only that it too will fall and rot without ever attaining its ultimate goal, the distant sun.

And the ideals flicker.

And the dream seems . . . naive . . .

Night. Under a pot of fresh-picked labrador tea, the campfire crackles and hisses. Cedar and balsam scent the air. Pine knots pop in a shower of sparks. Woodsmoke rises toward stars. And in the release of long-held sunlight glows an answer, so obvious, yet the culmination of a long search: Each twig, on every branch, from every tree, has long since stored the goal deep within itself. Each is filled with, was made to grow by, the ideal. In the act of reaching, it has already attained.

Though the goal seems out of reach, whispers the fire, though a thousand things of the world say, "It is not so," trust your own deepest instinct, your strongest yearning. The tree does not climb toward a sun that is not there. Believe it is so, act as if it *were* so, and it becomes so through you.

The pine knots pop and hiss, and the warmth of the campfire is enough. It is more than enough.

And if dreams are the seedlings of realities, it's through the cold winds of doubt, the hard rains of disappointment, and the rich soil of failure that they grow.

*The paddles whispers,
the canoe glides . . .*

$\mathcal{T}$his is the land of "glacial erratics"—huge boulders dropped by a retreating glacier some ten thousand years ago. Now they stand as mute sentinels from the past. They dream silently in the woods; they balance atop cliffs; they brood along lake shores.

Every stone has its own balancing point. How it has come to rest depends upon its size and shape, its unique weight and composition, its own personal history, and the lay of the land.

I am an erratic, too, I guess, with my own composition and personal history. My own balancing point. Like the boulders, I have been shaped and moved by forces beyond my control. Yet I am unlike the boulders in this: despite all the determining factors in my life, I am a being who can *choose*.

The choosing isn't easy. Taken together, the choices constitute a journey, an interconnected series of lakes and trails and rivers, dark woods and high overlooks. Sometimes the choices seem to stretch out like a long, blue horizon; at other times they are narrowed and constricted into a swift rapids. Here the current is strong, the obstacles many, but, once committed, there is no turning back. And even in the rapids, there are still choices, some freedom of movement within the swirling world of foam and rock. Cross draw, backpaddle, brace! Slide to the right to avoid the sweeper. Ferry across the current and pull an eddy turn for a short rest behind the big boulder. Now, straight through the standing waves at full bore!

There is always a choice. If only a choice of attitude.

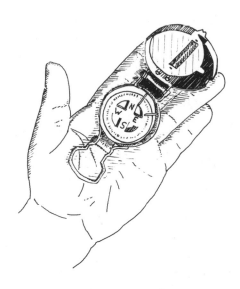

The whole of the universe is directed unerringly to one single individual—namely you.

—WALT WHITMAN

The paddle whispers,
the canoe glides . . .

*T*his pot is full. Full of fish chowder for supper. Potatoes, onions, dried milk, bits of boiled walleye . . . seasonings.

I like fish chowder. A lot. But this pot is full—if I want any more, I'll need a bigger pot.

This pot is full, too. Full of the ingredients that, altogether are . . . me. Some of the ingredients I like, some I don't. But the pot is *always* full, filled with whatever I am at the time. All of my emotions, strengths and weaknesses, journeys and memories are a part of the flavor, and, as long as I am here, nothing is poured out. To change the flavor, I can only add to the mix. In order to do that, I must choose to become . . . a *bigger pot.* Maybe I'll add a little more knowledge, a few more slices of patience, a dash of insight, a sprinkling of humor, the beauty of a sunset watched. I haven't really gotten rid of anything—ignorance, or impatience, selfishness or foolishness. I've simply added to the mix. I've chosen to be a bigger pot. I can also choose not to be.

I like fish chowder. Tomorrow night I use the bigger pot.

I've always been in love with pines. The massive, reaching limbs, the silhouettes, the way they cradle the stars at night. The smell of fallen needles carpeting the earth. When I was very young, the big pines looked to me as if they grew by simply grabbing ahold of the sky and hauling themselves up out of the earth.

Later, I learned some simple things about life. I'm still learning them. That pines . . . and dandelions and people . . . grow from where they are rooted. From the bottom up. From the inside out. That growth is slow. That grasping the air just means being toppled by the wind. That you don't hold onto the stars, but it's good to sometimes cradle them.

Growing seems to be a common trait among living things. But I wonder if anyone's ever done it better than an old pine.

If you're a pine, growth seems to have a lot to do with making the best of where you get started. Sometimes that's just a bare-bones, blustery, rocky outcrop of a place, inhospitable, with little soil or shelter, nurturing or encouragement. It may take a long time, but you somehow come to grips with it—this starting place. You reach and reach, stretching needy roots over naked granite, through tiny cracks, down into crevices. Until you finally find the footholds, the stability and sustenance you need. Then, someday, somehow, you transcend . . . growing up, while at the same time growing down, and growing out. Growing through all kinds of disasters. Growing *through* them.

And that's all there is to it, it seems. Grow. Down. Out. Up. Don't stop. Just grow.

Simple enough. But maybe it's the hardest, most important thing in the world. Maybe everything depends on it. Maybe the whole world depends on it.

If we were required to know the position of the fruit dots or the character of the endusium, nothing could be easier to ascertain, but if it is required that you be **affected** *by ferns, that they amount to anything, signify anything to you, that they be another sacred scripture and revelation to you, help to redeem your life, this end is not so easily accomplished.*

—HENRY DAVID THOREAU

*T*o notice the trembling of an aspen leaf at dawn; to dream dreams touched by night breezes and murmuring waves; to drink in the scents of the earth, of balm of Gilead or meadow-sweet; to paddle into the full hoop of a double rainbow and its reflection in a black lake; to catch the midnight howl of a wolf under the Corona Borealis, the wailing of loons echoing from a dark cliff; to sense . . . significance . . .

To begin to know a deepening awareness of each thought and action; to feel a unique separateness from, and interconnectedness with, all things . . .

Is there a name, a word for this process? Attention? Mindfulness? Consciousness? . . . Attunement.

And this, our life exempt from public haunt,
finds tongues in trees, books in the running
brooks, sermons in stones, and good in
everything.

—WILLIAM SHAKESPEARE

Going out ...

The old Lakota was wise. He knew that man's heart, away from nature, becomes hard; he knew that lack of respect for growing, living things soon led to lack of respect for humans too.

—LUTHER STANDING BEAR

Hurt not the earth, neither the sea, nor the trees.

—REVELATION 7:3

The fairest thing we can experience is the mysterious. It is the fundamental emotion at the cradle of true art and true science. He who knows it not is as good as dead, a snuffed-out candle . . .

—ALBERT EINSTEIN

If you understand, things are just as they are; if you do not understand, things are just as they are.

—ZEN VERSE

Part of this journey—maybe it's the whole thing—is that there is something here, something big—and small—that I am trying to be a part of. Or at least to understand, or just to touch. It's . . . the way the world works. The way things are. Reality.

Reality, right. And just what does that mean? Isn't each person's reality different from every other person's? And it's axiomatic that any human mind, being finite, cannot begin to know the infinite.

But maybe it's not done just with the mind, this knowing. Maybe it's also done with the feet—walking, standing; with the hands—holding, letting go; with the back—carrying; with the stomach—taking in other life, always life, making it me, experiencing the connection; with the skin—feeling cold, hot, wet, dry. Maybe that's why we're born with all these parts and not just a mind—the body is more than just a good container for a brain.

And maybe also the search to know the infinite, to eff the ineffable, finds the great through the small. Perhaps William Blake had it right when he said so beautifully—"To see the world in a grain of sand, and heaven in a wildflower, to hold infinity in the palm of your hand, eternity in an hour."

Well, there's plenty of sand here. And rock. And water and wildflowers and trees. Probably everything you'd need . . . But still, I don't think it can be done. I can't define reality. Not even my own reality. But maybe . . . by the process of elimination . . . I think I can say with some certainty what it's not. Reality, that is. A tree is not board feet. A river is not hydropower, nor is it a sewer. The sky is not just a good place for putting smokestacks, or for flying airplanes and getting faster, ever faster, from point A to point B. A wetland is not a missing wheat field. Fish are not fillets. Nothing is just raw material. The earth is not just a handy location for development and disposal. And . . . all the things and beings and people of the world are *not just what we can use them for.*

That's it, in reverse. What reality isn't. What it is, is . . . well, mystery. Evading the question? I don't think so. Because until we understand and appreciate elemental mystery, perhaps we can really understand or appreciate nothing else. If there are only uses and actions and observed results, then we miss the central fact, the pure wonder, of being. A tree is merely lumber. A mountain is a mine. A person is a consumer-producer. And life is . . . what? Just anticipated death?

That's not the way it's supposed to be. That's not life. That's not the way the world works. And maybe that's why we are called human beings—and not human doings.

My family—*Homo sapiens*—was born of a planet in which every stone was a teacher and a teaching, every breeze a language, every lake a mirror, and every tree a ladder to infinity. But we have worked so hard to redefine the world, turning all into a "commodity," human-made or human-used, that to a large extent we have succeeded. And now? . . . Now, all too often, life seems trivial and meaningless, precisely because we have so diligently removed or ignored all the meaning.

Man is whole when he is in tune with the winds, the stars, and the hills . . . Being in tune with the universe is the entire secret.

—Justice William O. Douglas

Along the way we have also removed the sweetness from the rain, the ozone from the sky, many of the great forests and wetlands and silences from the earth, and more and more of the species that are our relatives in this life. We have removed a great deal of the . . . reality.

As I look around me, I see the sapphire blue of sky and a sparkling lake, the green shades of trees, the swooping arcs of gulls, and the clean hardness of rocks. And I sense that only in opening my eyes wide enough to see that the world is a living poem and not dead matter, can I begin to know reality. Then I can embrace a real and natural world . . . that embraces me. And my family, my species—perhaps our salvation ultimately lies less in technology than in the simplicity of that timeless embrace—pondering a sunset, smelling a flower, planting a tree, beholding all life with wonder and reverence, and honoring the mysterious, beautiful poem of which we are a part.

The wonder of the world, the beauty and the power, the shapes of things, their colors, lights and shade. These I saw. Look ye also while life lasts.

From an old gravestone in
Cumberland, England
Favorite quote of F. Lee Jaques

162

And maybe, in the end, it is beauty itself that will save the world.

The paddle whispers,
the canoe glides . . .

A cool night. A bed of granite and caribou lichen, high above the silvered fastness of an untracked bog. A frog chorus rises and falls with the night breeze. To the west, a crescent moon dangles over pinnacled spruce. And overhead, stars and stars and stars and stars.

It's a wild, wild place, this universe—fresh-flavored and tart as a bog cranberry.

And what am I but a universe in miniature . . . with lakes and forests, stars and planets, undreamed of, and unexplored?

It seems I've always been listening for something—in early morning, in the hush of evening, along the trail and on the water. I've listened for a murmur, an undertone. A language, perhaps. Sometimes I've thought I heard . . . something. Spoken softly by the white-throat at dawn, or by the stream near which he sings; spoken by the wind in the pines and the rolling of distant night thunder; by mute sunrise and sunset, by the fragrant water lily or the spring hepatica.

Sometimes I believe I've heard the language, between and among and within this world of life and light, shape and substance. And if I tried to name it, the closest word would be—love. But even if I know its name, I understand it dimly, for it is heard *through* the senses, but *with* something deeper. I have found that to understand it, as with any language, means to listen. To listen means to stop. Become silent. Pay attention.

Having heard this language, I have also tried to speak it, and have been reminded of its hidden truth—that it is spoken not with your voice, but with your life.

*P*addling out. The last lake, the last crossing—sparkling, in a light wind. The last portage, the last carrying place. The spiraling song of a veery thrush, the "teacher-teacher" of an ovenbird, the smell of needles underfoot, the familiarity of rocks and moss and ferns. Then, finally, the journey home—to family and friends and responsibilities. The pots will be scrubbed and nested, one in the other, sleeping bag, pack, canoe, and paddles stored. For a time.

But they will not wait too long. Sooner than later, a few turns of the moon, and the trail will call again, and northern lights and loons and timelessness and beauty. And I will answer, and the paddle will pull the water, in a whisper . . .

Afterword

In a journey of discovery such as this, one travels alone. This has always been true. But it is only half true. The other half of the truth is that you *never* go alone. Alone, you come to meet the night sky, the sounds of wild things, fears, and doubts. You meet the universe alone. But in the search, in your pain and in your joy, you bring the past and future and all the world with you—into the meditation, into the voyage, into the vision quest. In your aloneness you *represent* the world; and what is found—secrets, dreams, stones, feathers, visions—though they may never be spoken of, they are brought back with you, through you, to the world.

The journey is not just for the journeyer, but for everyone. Thus it is real, and has meaning. Because each of us nourishes the world, as surely as each leaf nourishes the tree.

And the most secret of secrets, the one that whispers softest on the wind and clearest in the mind is this: Follow your heart into the heart of the wilderness, and you will find that it is not of herself alone that nature teaches, but of a wilderness more difficult to travel, a heart more difficult to know. Your own.

The quotations in this book have been islands and landmarks, or just points of beauty, along my way. Most are out of books, some came in letters from friends, others were jotted down on napkins, on the back of a hand, or on the bottom of a "to do" list. These are the authentic sources as nearly as I know.

St. Bernard de Clairvaux. *Epistles.* #106. 1115 A.D.

Walking Buffalo. From *Touch the Earth.* Compiled by T. C. McLuhan. New York: Outerbridge and Dienstfrey, 1971.

Sigurd F. Olson. *The Singing Wilderness.* New York: Alfred A. Knopf, 1956. Reprinted with permission.

Zen Forest: Sayings of the Masters. Translated by Soiku Shigematsu. Weatherhill, 1981.

John Muir. From the *The Wilderness World of John Muir.* Edited by Edwin Way Teale. Copyright © 1954, Edwin Way Teale, © renewed 1982 by Nellie D. Teale. Reprinted by permission of Houghton Mifflin Co. All rights reserved.

Old Inuit Song. From the movie *Never Cry Wolf.* Walt Disney Productions, 1983.

Helen Keller. *My Religion.* Doubleday & Co., 1927. The Swedenborg Foundation, Inc., 1960. Reprinted with permission.

Henry Wadsworth Longfellow. "The Harvest Moon."

Webster's New Collegiate Dictionary. G & C Merriam & Co., 1974.

Zen Haiku. From *Chop Wood, Carry Water.* Fields, Taylor, Weyler & Ingrasci. Los Angeles. Jeremy P. Tarcher Inc., 1984.

Percy Bysshe Shelley. "To Jane: The Invitation."

Isaiah 5:8. *The Bible, King James Version.*

Henry David Thoreau. *Walden.* 1854.

William Shakespeare. *As You Like It,* Act II.

Luther Standing Bear. From *Touch the Earth.* Compiled by T. C. McLuhan. New York: Outerbridge and Dienstfrey, 1971.

Revelation 7:3. *The Bible, King James Version.*

Albert Einstein. From *Living Philosophies,* Vol. 7., 1949.

Zen Verse. From *The Earth Speaks.* Compiled by Steve Van Matre and Bill Weiler, Warrenville, IN. Acclimatization Experiences Institute, 1983.

Justice William O. Douglas. *My Wilderness.* Doubleday, 1960.

Florence Page Jaques. *Frances Lee Jaques: Artist of the Wilderness World.* Doubleday, 1973.